oto by Shutterstock

American Homestead QUILTS

★ ★ ★ ★ ★ ★ ★

**Projects Inspired by
Iconic House Styles**

from Brownstone &
Saltbox
to Craftsman &
Farmhouse

Ellen Murphy

C&T PUBLISHING

Text copyright © 2014 by Ellen Murphy

Photography and Artwork copyright © 2014 by C&T Publishing, Inc.

Publisher: Amy Marson

Creative Director: Gailen Runge

Art Director: Kristy Zacharias

Editor: S. Michele Fry

Technical Editors: Ann Haley and Gailen Runge

Cover Designer: April Mostek

Book Designer: Christina Jarumay Fox

Production Coordinator: Rue Flaherty

Production Editor: Katie Van Amburg

Illustrator: Jenny Davis

Photo Assistant: Mary Peyton Peppo

Cover photography by Nissa Brehmer; Instructional photography by Diane Pedersen; Back cover style photography by Photospin and Shutterstock, unless otherwise noted

Published by C&T Publishing, Inc., P.O. Box 1456, Lafayette, CA 94549

Attention Teachers: C&T Publishing, Inc., encourages you to use this book as a text for teaching. Contact us at 800.284.1114 or www.ctpub.com for lesson plans and information about the C&T Creative Troupe.

We take great care to ensure that the information included in our products is accurate and presented in good faith, but no warranty is provided nor are results guaranteed. Having no control over the choices of materials or procedures used, neither the author nor C&T Publishing, Inc., shall have any liability to any person or entity with respect to any loss or damage caused directly or indirectly by the information contained in this book. For your convenience, we post an up-to-date listing of corrections on our website (www.ctpub.com). If a correction is not already noted, please contact our customer service department at ctinfo@ctpub.com or at P.O. Box 1456, Lafayette, CA 94549.

Trademark (™) and registered trademark (®) names are used throughout this book. Rather than use the symbols with every occurrence of a trademark or registered trademark name, we are using the names only in the editorial fashion and to the benefit of the owner, with no intention of infringement.

Library of Congress Cataloging-in-Publication Data

Murphy, Ellen, 1960-

  American homestead quilts : projects inspired by iconic house styles--from brownstone & saltbox to craftsman & farmhouse / Ellen Murphy

    pages cm

  ISBN 978-1-60705-807-6 (soft cover)

1. Quilting--Patterns. 2. Patchwork--Patterns. 3. Dwellings in art. I. Title.

  TT835.M473 2014

  746.46--dc23

                    2013027057

Printed in China

10 9 8 7 6 5 4 3 2 1

DEDICATION

*For those who share my American Homestead—
Robert, Katie Rose, Brennan,
and Mia the Wonder Dog*

ACKNOWLEDGMENTS

Thanks to my family for always encouraging my artistic pursuits, especially Mom, Dad, Mick, Trish, and Uncle Jamie.

Thanks to my friends who listen to my hopes and dreams at our "me time" sessions—Susan, Dawn, Irene, Maye, Donilyn, and Kate.

Thanks to the wonderful members of the Redbud Quilt Guild for all of the information I have learned from you through the years.

Thanks to Dawn from The Quilt Shoppe in Anderson, Indiana, for being my sounding board and quilt therapist, and for allowing me free use of all her wonderful collectibles.

Thanks to Shirley and Elsie for the inspiration for the Farmhouse quilt.

Thanks to Andover Fabrics and The Warm Company for their contributions to this book.

Thanks to my wonderful longarm quilters: Elaine Reed of Longarm Quilt'ER and Jennifer Cunningham of Wildflower Quilt Studio.

Thanks to C&T Publishing: from Amy and Gailen at my first venture in the quilting industry, to Roxane when the excitement of this dream became a reality, to Michele who taught me the new language of publishing, to Ann who made my quilts in her head, and to all the people who contributed to this book.

And special thanks to the inhabitants of my American Homestead—Avalon. To Robert, my Mr. Wonderful; my children, Katie Rose and Brennan; and Mia the Wonder Dog, my constant companion throughout this entire book. Thank you for always encouraging me to explore, dream, discover.

Contents

Introduction

From sea to shining sea, the United States is filled with a mix of American Homesteads. As I travel the world, I'm always struck by how unique the United States is. In many countries, the houses and lifestyles are similar from border to border. Not so in the United States. We have so many different landscapes, varied climates, and an eclectic mix of cultures coming together and blending into new family traditions. All that diversity is reflected in home styles and decor.

I should probably have a bumper sticker that says, "This Car Stops at House Tours." House tours, garden tours, historic homes—I love them all. I love to see how other people live, how they fashion their lives, how their possessions define them. It is fascinating to walk into a home and be able to know so much about people just by looking at how they decorate their homes. And many of these homes have quilts in them.

Sure, quilts are traditionally bed coverings, keeping people warm during the cold months. But they can be used all year, from enjoying a spring picnic in a wildflower meadow to watching fireworks on the beach in summer to bundling up on an autumn evening at a local football game to wrapping up in one in front of the fire during the first winter snowstorm.

They are also such magnificent works of art that they are often used all over the house as decor. Those pioneer women who sewed their scraps together could have just sewn things with no rhyme or reason, making something just to provide warmth. But instead, they fashioned those scraps into intricate patterns. The quilts were expressions of their artistic abilities. I'm sure those quilters were as proud of their work as we are of ours today. And happily today, we find quilts all over the house, from a lap quilt draped on a sofa to table runners in the dining room to stunning quilts that hang on the wall as the focal point of a room.

So come join us as we look at a selection of quilts and take a house tour of home styles across the United States.

From my American Homestead to wherever you may call home,

All the best,

Ellen

Helpful Hints

SEAMS

Scant ¼": All the seams should be sewn with a scant ¼" seam. That's about a pencil-line's width narrower than ¼". A scant seam makes pieces fit together and line up correctly.

Locking the Seams: To ensure precise piecing, I have provided specific directions for pressing the seams, as this will ensure that your points come out perfectly. It is easy to do and well worth the fussing in the beginning.

Reducing Bulk: In pieced quilts, which have lots of fabric pieces coming together in a tiny area, consider pressing your seams open. Whenever you can make those seam intersections lie flatter, you will have a better chance of reducing distortion in your piecing and machine quilting. If your machine hits a large clump of fabric, it can jar your line of stitching off course. Please don't think I'm telling you to press open every seam—No! In this book, I'll instruct you when to press open a seam.

STRIP PIECING

When strip piecing, or sewing long strips together on the long edge of the fabric, start sewing each new seam from the opposite end as the previous seam. I keep my beginning thread tails in place to remind me where I started the previous seam. Beginning on alternate ends will keep the unit square; otherwise the fabric could bow and arc, and you will not be able to cut it easily. Press the seams toward the darker fabric. Square up one end and cut sections as stated in your pattern. Be careful to keep the units square; if you see they are not square, square up a small section and begin again.

SQUARING UP

No matter how careful you may be as a quilter, you are working with fabric, and it moves! It is easier to square up each unit as you go along. This gives you a better chance of a precise final project.

MAKING A DOUBLE-FOLD BINDING

1. Trim excess batting and backing from the quilt so they are even with the edges of the quilt top.

2. If you want a ¼" finished binding, cut the binding strips 2" wide and piece them together with diagonal seams to make a continuous binding strip. Trim the seam allowance to ¼". Press the seams open.

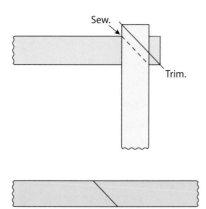

3. Press the entire strip in half lengthwise with wrong sides together. With raw edges even, pin the binding to the front edge of the quilt a few inches from a corner, and leave the first few inches of the binding unattached. Start sewing, using a ¼" seam allowance.

4. Stop ¼" away from the first corner (Figure A), and backstitch 1 stitch. Lift the presser foot and needle. Rotate the quilt a quarter turn. Fold the binding at a right angle so it extends straight above the quilt and the fold forms a 45° angle in the corner (Figure B). Then bring the binding strip down so it is even with the edge of the quilt (Figure C). Begin sewing at the folded edge. Repeat in the same manner at all corners.

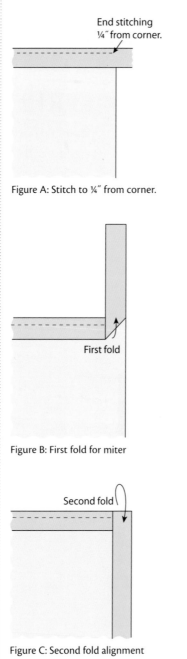

Figure A: Stitch to ¼" from corner.

Figure B: First fold for miter

Figure C: Second fold alignment

5. Continue stitching until you are back near the beginning of the binding strip.

6. Fold the ending tail of the binding back on itself where it meets the beginning binding tail. From the fold, measure and mark the cut width of your binding strip. Cut the ending binding tail to this measurement. For example, if your binding is cut 2" wide, measure from the fold on the ending tail of the binding 2" and cut the binding tail to this length.

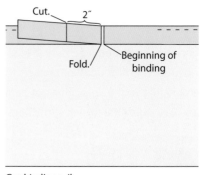

Cut binding tail.

7. Open both tails. Place 1 tail on top of the other tail at right angles, right sides together. Mark a diagonal line from corner to corner and stitch on the line. Check that you've done it correctly and that the binding fits the quilt; then trim the seam allowance to ¼". Press open.

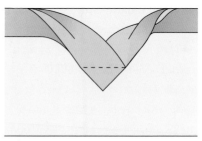

Stitch ends of binding diagonally.

8. Refold the binding and stitch this binding section in place on the quilt. Fold the binding over the raw edges to the quilt back, and hand stitch.

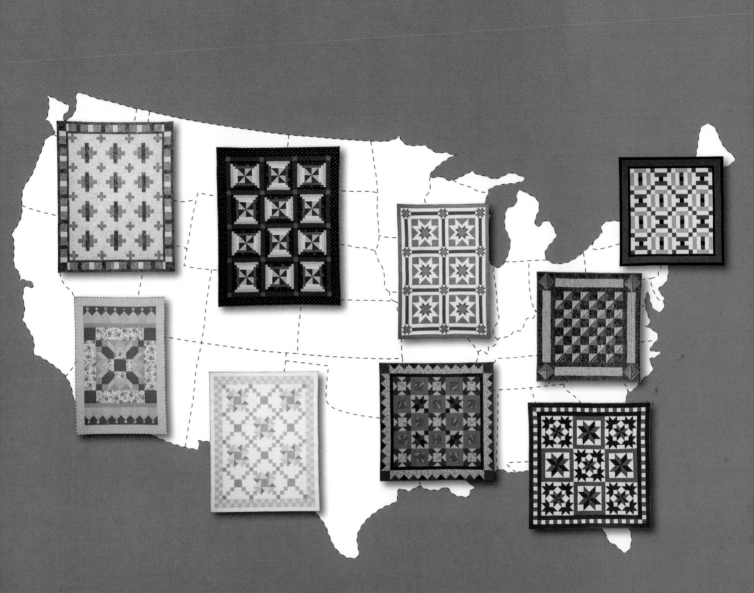

MAP 7

Photo by Avalon

Photo by Avalon

AMERICAN HOMESTEAD QUILTS

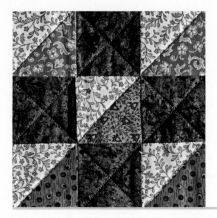

Colonial Saltbox

O n a tree-lined street in a historic village stands a house older than the United States itself. Built before the American Revolution, this saltbox house has witnessed relationships among new settlers, seen future presidents playing in the neighborhood, and suffered redcoats marching through. The present owners embrace its historic roots and furnish it in Colonial style, including this quilt inspired by a colonial game board.

Designed, pieced, and quilted by Ellen Murphy

Finished quilt: 24½″ × 24½″

MATERIALS

Fabric A (green): ½ yard

Fabric B (beige): ½ yard

Fabrics C–J (assorted cheddars):
8 fabrics, ¼ yard each

Binding (cheddar): ¼ yard

Backing: 1 yard

Batting: 30″ × 30″ square

CUTTING

Fabric A

- Cut 32 squares 2½″ × 2½″.

- Cut 8 squares 3¼″ × 3¼″.

- Cut 8 strips 1½″ × 16½″.

Fabric B

- Cut 16 squares 3¼″ × 3¼″.

- Cut 4 strips 2½″ × 16½″.

Fabrics C–J

- Cut 3 squares 3¼″ × 3¼″ from each fabric.

Backing

- Cut 1 square 30″ × 30″.

MAKE THE HALF-SQUARE TRIANGLES

1. Mark a diagonal line on the wrong side of the 8 Fabric A 3¼″ × 3¼″ squares and 16 Fabric B squares.

2. Place a Fabric A square from Step 1 right sides together with a Fabric C square. Repeat to pair a Fabric A square with each of the Fabric D–J squares to make 8 pairs. In a similar fashion, pair a Fabric B square from Step 1 with each of the remaining C–J squares to make 16 squares.

3. For each pair from Step 2, sew ¼″ away from each side of the drawn diagonal line. Cut on the drawn line. Press the seams as follows:

- For the 16 half-square triangles with Fabric A, press the seam allowance in the 8 A/D, A/F, A/H, and A/J squares toward Fabric A. Press the seam allowance in the remaining 8 A/C, A/E, A/G, and A/I squares toward Fabrics C, E, G, and I, as shown in the illustrations for Make the Corner Units, Step 1 (at right).

- For all of the Fabric B half-square triangles, press the seam allowance toward Fabrics C–J.

4. Square each half-square triangle to 2½″ × 2½″. (These will be used for the corner and center units.)

MAKE THE CORNER UNITS

1. Lay out the corner units as shown, paying attention to the arrows that show the direction of the seam allowance. The corner units utilize the 16 half-square triangles with Fabric A. For each corner unit, sew 4 half-square triangles together in 2 rows as shown, making sure to *lock* the diagonal seams. (Refer to Locking the Seams, page 5.) Press the seam in Row 1 to the left and the seam in Row 2 to the right.

Make 2.

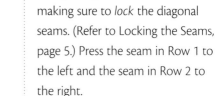

Make 2.

2. Sew the rows together to make 4 corner units, making sure to lock the seams again. Press the final seams open to reduce bulk.

3. Square each corner unit to 4½″ × 4½″, if needed.

MAKE THE BORDER UNITS

1. Place a Fabric A strip on either side of a Fabric B strip and stitch together along the long edges. Be sure to reverse your starting sides (see Strip Piecing, page 5). Press the seams open to reduce bulk.

2. Square up the border unit to 4½" × 16½".

3. Repeat Steps 1 and 2 to make 4 units. Set aside.

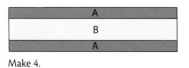

Make 4.

MAKE THE CENTER UNIT

1. Place the Fabric A 2½" squares and Fabric B half-square triangles in 8 rows as shown. Sew the units together to make 8 rows. Press the seams in Rows 1, 3, 5, and 7 to the left. Press the seams in Rows 2, 4, 6, and 8 to the right.

2. Sew the rows together, being sure to lock the opposing seams together. Begin to sew each row from alternate sides (see Strip Piecing, page 5). Press each of these seams open to reduce bulk.

3. Square the center unit to 16½" × 16½".

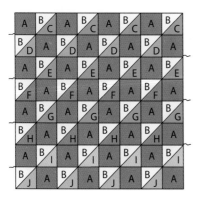

ASSEMBLE THE QUILT

1. Lay out the center, border, and corner units as shown and sew them together in 3 rows. For the top and bottom rows, add a corner unit to either end of a border unit (see illustration, below). For the middle row, sew a border unit to each side of the center unit. Press the seams in Rows 1 and 3 to the inside and the seams in Row 2 to the outside.

2. Sew the rows together; press the final seams open to reduce bulk.

3. Square the quilt top to 24½" × 24½".

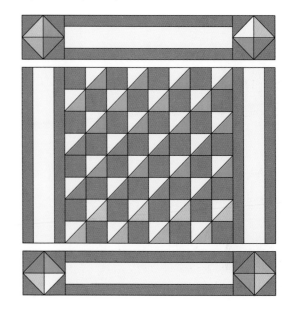

QUILTING

Layer the backing, batting, and quilt top. Quilt as desired.

BINDING

1. Cut 3 strips 2" × width of fabric (selvage to selvage) from the binding fabric.

2. Bind the quilt (see Making a Double-Fold Binding, page 6).

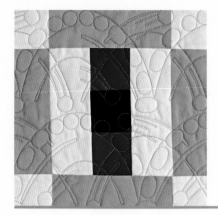

City Brownstone

She lives in a major metropolis, not far from the subway, with views of skyscrapers and bridges. But her home is in a friendly neighborhood, where residents buy fruit from a corner market after they've had dinner at a family-owned pizza place. Distancing herself further from the hustle and bustle, she arrives home to her collection of American folk art pieces that are traditional with a modern twist—like the quilt her little sister made especially for her.

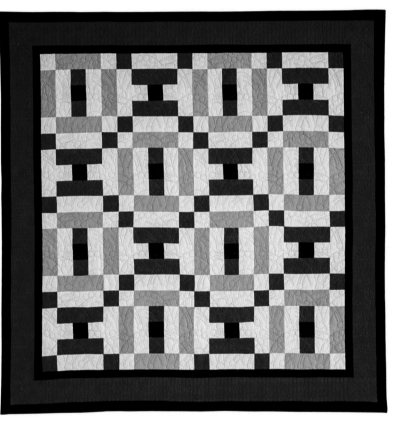

Designed and pieced by Ellen Murphy, quilted by Elaine Reed

Finished quilt: 50½″ × 50½″

Finished block: 10″ × 10″

MATERIALS

Fabric A (white): 1 yard

Fabric B (red): 1¼ yards

Fabric C (gray): ⅝ yard

Fabric D (black): ¾ yard

Backing: 3½ yards (or 1¾ yards extra-wide quilt backing)

Batting: 58″ × 58″

Binding: ½ yard

BLOCK 1

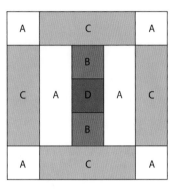

CUTTING

Fabric A
- Cut 32 squares 2½″ × 2½″.
- Cut 16 rectangles 2½″ × 6½″.

Fabric B
- Cut 16 squares 2½″ × 2½″.

Fabric C
- Cut 32 rectangles 2½″ × 6½″.

Fabric D
- Cut 8 squares 2½″ × 2½″.

MAKE THE BLOCK 1 CENTER

1. Sew a Fabric B square to either side of a Fabric D square. Press the seams toward the center square.

2. Stitch a Fabric A rectangle to each side of the unit from Step 1. Press the seams toward the center. Square to 6½″ × 6½″.

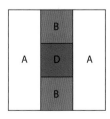

3. Repeat Steps 1 and 2 to make a total of 8 Block 1 centers.

ASSEMBLE BLOCK 1

1. Lay out units as shown and sew together in 3 rows. Press the seams toward Fabric C.

2. Sew the rows together. Press the seams to the outside.

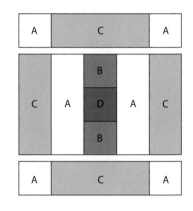

3. Square the block to 10½″ × 10½″.

4. Repeat Steps 1–3 to complete 8 of Block 1.

BLOCK 2

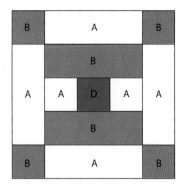

CUTTING

Fabric A

- Cut 16 squares 2½″ × 2½″.

- Cut 32 rectangles 2½″ × 6½″.

Fabric B

- Cut 32 squares 2½″ × 2½″.

- Cut 16 rectangles 2½″ × 6½″.

Fabric D

- Cut 8 squares 2½″ × 2½″.

MAKE THE BLOCK 2 CENTER

1. Stitch a Fabric A square to each side of a Fabric D square. Press the seams toward the center square.

2. Stitch a Fabric B rectangle to each side of the unit from Step 1. Press the seams to the outside.

3. Square the block center to 6½″ × 6½″.

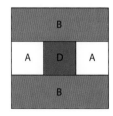

4. Repeat Steps 1–3 to make 8 Block 2 center units.

ASSEMBLE BLOCK 2

1. Lay out the units as shown and sew together in 3 rows. Press the seams in Rows 1 and 3 to the outside and the seams in Row 2 to the inside.

2. Sew the rows together and press the seams toward the center of the block.

3. Square the block to 10½″ × 10½″.

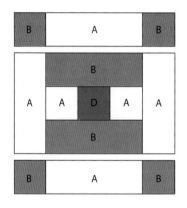

4. Repeat Steps 1–3 to complete 8 of Block 2.

ASSEMBLE THE QUILT CENTER

1. Lay out the blocks as shown and sew together to form 4 rows. Press the seams in Rows 1 and 3 to the left and the seams in Rows 2 and 4 to the right.

2. Sew the rows together and press the seams open to reduce bulk.

BORDERS

INNER BORDER

1. Cut 5 strips 1½" × width of fabric (selvage to selvage) from Fabric D. Stitch the strips together end to end.

2. Measure the quilt top from top to bottom through the middle. Cut 2 strips to this length. Sew a strip to each side of the quilt; press the seams toward the border.

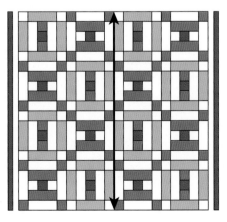

3. Measure the quilt top from side to side, including borders added in Step 2. Cut 2 strips to this length. Sew a strip to the top and bottom of the quilt; press the seams toward the border.

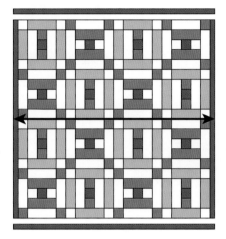

MIDDLE BORDER

1. Cut 5 strips 3½" × width of fabric (selvage to selvage) from Fabric B. Stitch the strips together end to end.

2. Follow Steps 2 and 3 for Inner Border (at left and above) to trim and stitch the middle border strips to the sides, top, and bottom of the quilt top.

OUTER BORDER

1. Cut 5 strips 1½" × width of fabric (selvage to selvage) from Fabric D. Stitch the strips together end to end.

2. Follow Steps 2 and 3 for Inner Border (page 16) to trim and stitch the outer border strips to the sides, top, and bottom of the quilt top.

QUILTING

Layer the backing, batting, and quilt top. Quilt as desired.

BINDING

1. Cut 6 strips 2" × width of fabric (selvage to selvage) from the binding fabric.

2. Bind the quilt (see Making a Double-Fold Binding, page 6).

Photo by Photospin

Photo by Avalon

Photo by C&T Publishing

Beach House

The busiest time of the year for this beach house is Independence Day. The family invites any and all extended family members to come for a visit. A home usually decorated nautically takes on a less stylish and more lived-in look with beach balls, flip-flops, swim-suits, towels, and tubes of sunscreen all around. And sand. There's always sand. This quilt, inspired by the holiday, never touches the sand, but it does bring its own brand of fireworks to the decor.

Designed and pieced by Ellen Murphy, quilted by Jennifer Cunningham

Finished quilt: 60½″ × 60½″

Finished block: 16″ × 16″

Fabric A (white): 2 yards

Fabric B (blue): 2¼ yards

Fabric C (red): 1½ yards

Backing: 4 yards (or 2 yards extra-wide backing)

Batting: 68″ × 68″

Binding: ⅝ yard

BLOCK 1

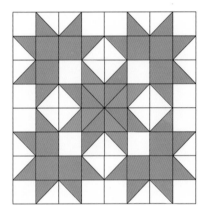

CUTTING

Fabric A
- Cut 80 squares 2½″ × 2½″.
- Cut 80 squares 3¼″ × 3¼″.

Fabric B
- Cut 60 squares 2½″ × 2½″.
- Cut 80 squares 3¼″ × 3¼″.

Fabric C
- Cut 20 squares 3¼″ × 3¼″.

MAKE THE HALF-SQUARE TRIANGLES

1. Mark a diagonal line on the wrong side of each Fabric A 3¼″ × 3¼″ square and each Fabric C square.

2. Pair the 3¼″ × 3¼″ squares with right sides together in the following combinations:

- 70 A/B pairs
- 10 B/C pairs
- 10 A/C pairs

3. For each pair, sew ¼″ away from each side of the diagonal line; cut on the drawn line.

4. Press the seams as follows:

- 140 A/B half-square triangles— Press the seams in 80 A/B half-square triangles toward Fabric A. Press the seams in 60 A/B half-square triangles toward Fabric B.

- 20 B/C half-square triangles—Press the seams toward Fabric C.

- 20 A/C half-square triangles—Press the seams toward Fabric C.

5. Square each half-square triangle from Step 4 to 2½″ × 2½″.

MAKE THE QUARTER UNIT SECTIONS

Sections 1–4

1. Lay out the pieces as shown and sew them together in 2 rows. Press the seams in Row 1 to the left and the seams in Row 2 to the right. Pay attention to the arrows, which show the direction of the seams in the half-square triangles.

Section 1

Section 2

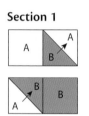

Section 3

Section 4

2. Sew the rows together and press the seams in sections 1 and 3 to the bottom and the seams in sections 2 and 4 to the top. Square each section to 4½″ × 4½″.

3. Repeat Steps 1 and 2 to make 20 of each section.

ASSEMBLE THE QUARTER UNITS

1. Lay out the sections as shown. Sew them together in 2 rows. Press the seam in Row 1 to the left and the seam in Row 2 to the right.

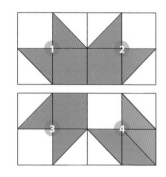

2. Sew the rows together. Press the seam to the top. Square the quarter unit to 8½″ × 8½″.

3. Repeat Steps 1 and 2 to make 20 quarter units.

ASSEMBLE BLOCK 1

1. Lay out the quarter units as shown (rotate units so the B/C half-square triangle is in the middle of block). Sew them together in 2 rows. Press the seam in Row 1 to the right and the seam in Row 2 to the left.

2. Sew the rows together. Press the final seam open to reduce bulk. Square the block to 16½″ × 16½″.

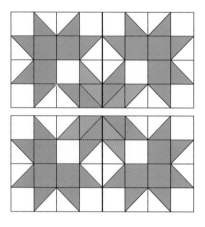

3. Repeat Steps 1 and 2 to make 5 of Block 1.

BLOCK 2

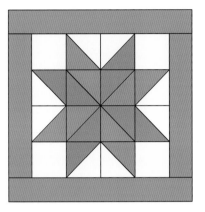

CUTTING

Fabric A

- Cut 16 squares 3½″ × 3½″.

- Cut 16 squares 4¼″ × 4¼″.

Fabric B

- Cut 16 squares 4¼″ × 4¼″.

Fabric C

- Cut 16 squares 4¼″ × 4¼″.

- Cut 8 strips 2½″ × 12½″.

- Cut 8 strips 2½″ × 16½″.

MAKE THE HALF-SQUARE TRIANGLES

1. Draw a diagonal line on the wrong side of each Fabric A 4¼″ × 4¼″ square and each Fabric C square.

2. Pair the 4¼″ × 4¼″ squares with right sides together in the following combinations:

- 8 A/C pairs

- 8 A/B pairs

- 8 B/C pairs

3. For each pair, sew ¼″ away from each side of the drawn line; cut on the drawn line.

4. Press the seams as follows:

- 8 A/C half-square triangles—Press the seams toward Fabric A.

- 8 A/B half-square triangles—Press the seams toward Fabric B.

- 8 C/B half-square triangles—Press the seams toward Fabric B.

5. Square each half-square triangle from Step 4 to 3½″ × 3½″.

MAKE THE QUARTER UNITS

1. Lay out the pieces as shown and sew together in 2 rows. Press the seams in Row 1 to the right and the seams in Row 2 to the left.

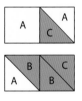

2. Sew the rows together and press the seam to the top.

3. Square the quarter unit to 6½″ × 6½″.

4. Repeat Steps 1–3 to make 16 quarter units.

ASSEMBLE THE INNER BLOCKS

1. Lay out the quarter units as shown. Rotate the units so the B/C half-square triangle is in the middle of the block. Sew them together in 2 rows; press the seam in Row 1 to the left and the seam in Row 2 to the right.

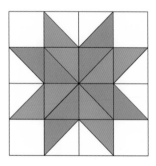

2. Sew the rows together. Press the final seam open to reduce bulk.

3. Square the block center to 12½" × 12½".

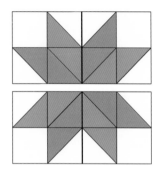

4. Sew a Fabric C 2½" × 12½" strip to each side of the block center; press the seams to the outside.

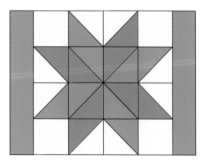

5. Sew a Fabric C 2½" × 16½" strip to the top and bottom of the block; press the seams to the outside. Square the block to 16½" × 16½".

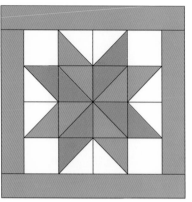

6. Repeat Steps 1–5 to make 4 of Block 2.

ASSEMBLE THE QUILT CENTER

1. Lay out the blocks as shown and sew together in 3 rows. Press the seams in Rows 1 and 3 to the inside and the seams in Row 2 to the outside.

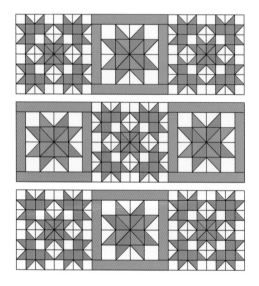

2. Sew the rows together and press the seams open to reduce bulk.

BORDERS

INNER BORDER

1. Cut 6 strips 2½" × width of fabric from Fabric B. Stitch the strips together end to end.

2. Measure the quilt top from top to bottom through the middle. Cut 2 strips to this length. Sew a strip to either side of the quilt top. Press the seams to the outside.

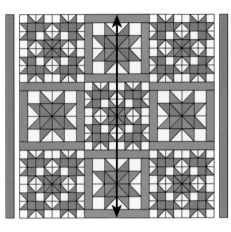

3. Measure the quilt top from side to side, including borders added in Step 2, through the middle. Cut 2 strips to this length. Sew a strip to the top and bottom of the quilt top. Press the seams to the outside.

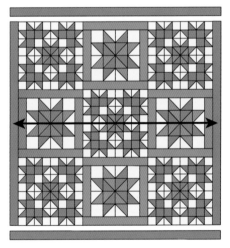

CHECKED BORDER

1. Cut 4 strips 2½" × width of fabric from Fabric A.

2. Cut 4 strips 2½" × width of fabric from Fabric C.

3. Lay out the strips as shown and stitch the long edges together (see Strip Piecing, page 5).

4. Square up the left edge as shown. Cross cut the strip set into 14 units, each 2½" wide.

5. Separate a unit from Step 4 into 2 sections as shown, discarding 2 of the squares. Repeat with a second unit from Step 4.

6. Arrange some of the units from Steps 4 and 5 as shown. Stitch the units together to make a side border. Repeat to make 2 side borders.

7. Noting the color placement, stitch a side border from Step 6 to either side of the quilt.

8. Arrange additional units from Steps 4 and 5 as shown. Stitch the units together to make the top border. Repeat to make an identical border for the bottom.

9. Noting the color placement, stitch a border from Step 8 to the top and bottom of the quilt.

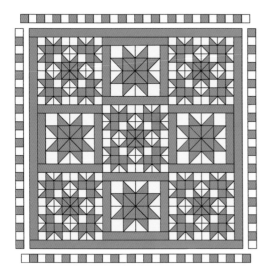

OUTER BORDER

1. Cut 6 strips 2½″ × width of fabric from Fabric B. Stitch the strips together end to end.

2. Measure and trim the long strip from Step 1 as you did in Inner Border (page 24). Begin by measuring the quilt top from top to bottom through the middle. Cut 2 strips to this length. Sew a strip to each side of the quilt; press the seams to the outside. Measure the quilt top from side to side, including borders, through the middle. Cut 2 strips to this length. Sew a strip to the top and bottom of quilt; press the seams to the outside.

QUILTING

Layer the backing, batting, and quilt top. Quilt as desired.

BINDING

1. Cut 7 strips 2″ × width of fabric (selvage to selvage) from the binding fabric.

2. Bind the quilt (see Making a Double-Fold Binding, page 6).

Photo by Shutterstock

Photo by Avalon

Photo by Avalon

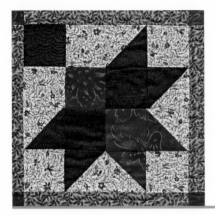

Historic Plantation

This grand house is a fine example of historic preservation. Seeking to ensure that the house and its long history endure for many generations to come, the owners have had it added to historic registries and have opened it for tours. They are no longer alone in fighting the time and kudzu that continually attempt to over-take their space. And they preserve the antebellum style. The plantation shutters on the tall French windows once helped keep the house ever-so-slightly cooler; now they protect the antiques from sun damage. The lifestyle is much different from what it was in eighteenth- and nineteenth-century days, but guests can still enjoy a sweet tea on the wraparound porch as the scent of magnolia, sweet and heavy, floats on the warm Southern breezes.

Designed and pieced by Ellen Murphy, quilted by Elaine Reed
Most fabric from the Sentiments collection by 3 Sisters for Moda

Finished quilt: 52½″ × 52½″

Finished block: 8″ × 8″

MATERIALS

Fabric A (off-white): ¾ yard

Fabric B (red): 1⅓ yards

Fabric C (red paisley): ⅓ yard

Fabric D (light green): ⅞ yard

Fabric E (dark green): 1⅛ yards

Fabric F (cream paisley): ⅓ yard

Fabric G (light green floral): 1 yard

Backing: 3½ yards (or 1¾ yards extra-wide quilt backing)

Batting: 60″ × 60″

Binding: ½ yard

BLOCK 1

CUTTING

Fabric C
- Cut 12 squares 4½″ × 4½″.

Fabric D
- Cut 24 rectangles 2½″ × 4½″.
- Cut 24 rectangles 2½″ × 8½″.

ASSEMBLE BLOCK 1

1. Sew a Fabric D 2½″ × 4½″ rectangle to each side of a Fabric C square. Press toward the center square.

2. Sew a Fabric D 2½″ × 8½″ rectangle to the top and bottom of the unit from Step 1. Square to 8½″ × 8½″. Press away from the center.

3. Repeat Steps 1 and 2 to make 12 of Block 1.

BLOCK 2

CUTTING

Fabric A
- Cut 36 rectangles 2½″ × 4½″.

Fabric B
- Cut 108 squares 2½″ × 2½″.

Fabric F
- Cut 9 squares 4½″ × 4½″.

MAKE THE FLYING GEESE UNITS

1. Draw a diagonal line from corner to corner on the wrong side of 72 Fabric B squares.

2. Place a Fabric B square from Step 1 on the left side of a Fabric A rectangle, right sides together. Sew a thread-width below the drawn line.

3. Trim the seam allowance to ¼″. Open the top piece and press the seam toward the corner.

4. Repeat Steps 1–3 on the right side of the square as shown.

5. Square the Flying Geese unit to 2½″ × 4½″.

6. Repeat Steps 1–5 to make 36 Flying Geese units.

ASSEMBLE BLOCK 2

1. Lay out the units with a Flying Geese unit on each side of a Fabric F square as shown. Place a Fabric B square in each corner. Sew the units into rows. Press the seams in Rows 1 and 3 to the outside and the seams in Row 2 to the inside.

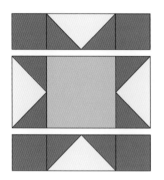

2. Sew the rows together. Press the seams toward the center.

3. Square the block to 8½″ × 8½″.

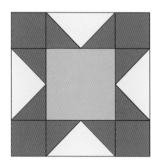

4. Repeat Steps 1–3 to make 9 of Block 2.

BLOCK 3

CUTTING

Fabric A
- Cut 20 squares 2½″ × 2½″.
- Cut 12 squares 3¼″ × 3¼″.

Fabric B
- Cut 8 squares 2½″ × 2½″.
- Cut 4 squares 3¼″ × 3¼″.

Fabric E
- Cut 12 squares 2½″ × 2½″.
- Cut 8 squares 3¼″ × 3¼″.

MAKE THE HALF-SQUARE TRIANGLES

1. Draw a diagonal line from corner to corner on the wrong side of 12 Fabric A 3¼″ × 3¼″ squares.

2. Pair the 3¼″ × 3¼″ squares with right sides together in the following combinations:
- 4 A/B pairs
- 8 A/E pairs

3. Sew ¼″ on either side of the drawn line. Cut on the drawn line. Press the seams as follows:
- Press the A/B half-square triangles toward Fabric A.
- Press the A/E half-square triangles toward Fabric E.

4. Square each half-square triangle to 2½″ × 2½″.

ASSEMBLE BLOCK 3

1. Lay out the units as shown and sew together in 4 rows. Press the seams in Rows 1 and 3 to the left and the seams in Rows 2 and 4 to the right.

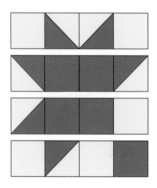

2. Stitch the rows together. Press the seams open to reduce bulk. Square to 8½″ × 8½″.

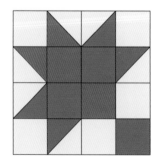

3. Repeat Steps 1 and 2 to make 4 of Block 3.

MAKE THE QUILT CENTER

Arrange the blocks into rows, rotating Block 3, as shown. Stitch together in 5 rows. Press the seams in Rows 1, 3, and 5 to the left and the seams in Rows 2 and 4 to the right. Sew the rows together and press the final seams open to reduce bulk.

BORDERS

INNER BORDER

1. Cut 5 strips 2″ × width of fabric from Fabric E. Stitch the strips together end to end.

2. Measure the quilt top from top to bottom through the middle. Cut 2 strips to this length. Stitch a strip to either side of the quilt top. Press the seams toward the border.

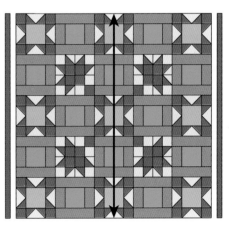

3. Measure the quilt top from side to side, including borders added in Step 2. Cut 2 strips to this length. Stitch a strip to the top and bottom of the quilt top. Press the seams toward the border.

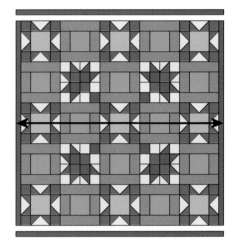

OUTER BORDER

1. Cut 4 squares 5″ × 5″ from Fabric B.

2. Cut 5 strips 5″ × width of fabric from Fabric G. Stitch the strips together end to end.

3. Measure the quilt top from top to bottom through the middle. Cut 4 strips to this length.

4. Stitch a strip from Step 3 to either side of the quilt top. Press the seams toward the borders.

5. Sew a 5″ × 5″ Fabric B square to either end of the remaining 2 strips from Step 3. Press the seams toward the border strip.

6. Stitch the border/corner units from Step 5 to the top and bottom of the quilt top, matching the seams. Press the seams toward the borders.

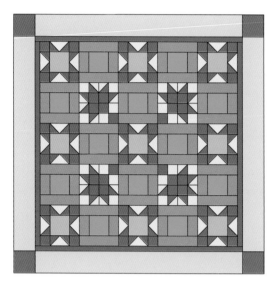

MAKE THE PRAIRIE POINTS

1. Cut 20 squares 5″ × 5″ from Fabric B. Cut 20 squares 5″ × 5″ from Fabric E.

2. Fold a 5″ × 5″ square from Step 1 in half with wrong sides together as shown. Press.

3. Fold each upper corner to the center of the open edge and press.

4. Repeat Steps 2 and 3 with all B and E squares from Step 1 to make 40 prairie points. Set aside.

QUILTING

Layer the backing, batting, and quilt top. Quilt as desired.

PRAIRIE POINT PLACEMENT

Evenly place 10 prairie points along each outside edge of the quilt between the corner squares. Be sure to alternate colors as shown; prairie points will overlap a bit. Pin in place, and then baste ⅛″ from the raw edges.

BINDING

1. Cut 6 strips 2″ × width of fabric (selvage to selvage) from the binding fabric.

2. Bind the quilt (see Making a Double-Fold Binding, page 6).

Photo by Shutterstock

Photo by Axolotl

Photo by

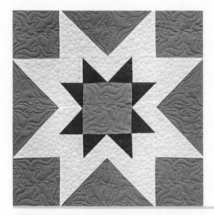

Farmhouse

This historic homestead has been in the same family for more than 100 years. Three generations have filled the house with memories and mementos. Back in the day, sheep, cows, and pigs roamed the acres that weren't sown with corn and soybeans. Now the family owns fewer acres, but those acres grow the best organic produce in the county. Locals line up early on harvest days to get corn, tomatoes, and peppers fresh from the field. The family booth is a favorite at the weekly farmer's market. Although the whole household doesn't work the land these days, this house is still home—a respite where everyone enjoys the wide-open views; dark, quiet nights; and the authenticity of country living. This example of Americana lifestyle inspired a quilt that is both useful and decorative in this home.

Designed and pieced by Ellen Murphy, quilted by Jennifer Cunningham

Finished quilt: 54½″ × 76½″

Finished block: 16″ × 16″

Fabric A (turquoise): 2⅛ yards

Fabric B (white): 3 yards

Fabric C (red): 1½ yards

Backing: 4¾ yards (or 1¾ yards extra-wide quilt backing)

Batting: 62″ × 84″

Binding (red): ⅝ yard

BLOCKS

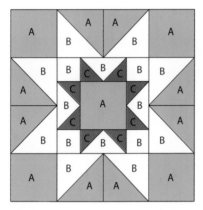

CUTTING

Fabric A

■ Cut 30 squares 4½″ × 4½″.

■ Cut 24 squares 5¼″ × 5¼″.

Fabric B

■ Cut 24 squares 5¼″ × 5¼″.

■ Cut 24 squares 2½″ × 2½″.

■ Cut 24 rectangles 2½″ × 4½″.

Fabric C

■ Cut 48 squares 2½″ × 2½″.

MAKE THE FLYING GEESE UNITS

1. Mark a diagonal line from corner to corner on the wrong side of the Fabric C squares.

2. Place a Fabric C square on the left side of a Fabric B rectangle, right sides together. Sew a thread-width below the drawn line.

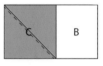

3. Trim the seam allowance to ¼″. Open the top piece and press the seam toward the corner.

4. Repeat Steps 2 and 3 on the right side of the rectangle.

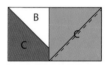

5. Square the Flying Geese unit to 2½″ × 4½″.

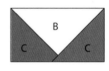

6. Repeat Steps 2–5 to make 24 Flying Geese units.

ASSEMBLE THE CENTER STAR

1. Arrange a Fabric A 4½″ × 4½″ square, 4 Flying Geese units, and 4 Fabric B 2½″ × 2½″ squares to form a center star, as shown. Stitch together in 3 rows. Press the seams in Rows 1 and 3 to the outside and the seams in Row 2 to the inside.

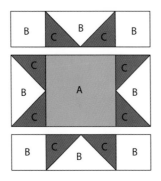

2. Sew the rows together. Press the seams open to reduce bulk.

3. Repeat Steps 1 and 2 to make 6 center stars.

COMPLETE THE BLOCKS

MAKE THE HALF-SQUARE TRIANGLES

1. Draw a diagonal line from corner to corner on the wrong side of 24 Fabric B 5¼″ × 5¼″ squares.

2. Pair a Fabric A 5¼″ × 5¼″ square with a Fabric B 5¼″ × 5¼″ square, right sides together.

3. Stitch ¼″ from either side of the drawn line. Cut on the drawn line.

4. Repeat Steps 2 and 3 to make 48 A/B half-square triangles. Press the seams of 24 of the A/B half-square triangles toward Fabric A and the seams of the remaining 24 half-square triangles toward Fabric B.

5. Square each half-square triangle to 4½″ × 4½″.

MAKE THE OUTER MIDDLE UNITS

Lay out 2 A/B half-square triangles as shown, paying attention to the arrows indicating the pressing direction. Stitch the half-square triangles together, and press the seam open. Repeat to make 24 units.

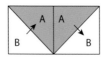

ASSEMBLE THE BLOCK

1. Arrange the block pieces as shown. Stitch the pieces together in 3 rows. Press the seams in Rows 1 and 3 to the outside and the seams in Row 2 to the inside.

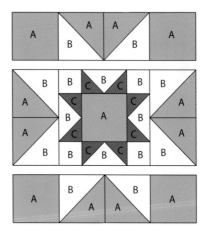

2. Sew the rows together and press the final seams open to reduce bulk.

3. Repeat Steps 1 and 2 to make 6 blocks.

MAKE THE CORNER BLOCKS

Fabric A

- Cut 12 squares 3½″ × 3½″.

Fabric B

- Cut 48 squares 2″ × 2″.

- Cut 48 rectangles 2″ × 3½″.

Fabric C

- Cut 96 squares 2″ × 2″.

MAKE THE FLYING GEESE UNITS

1. Draw a diagonal line from corner to corner on the wrong side of 96 Fabric C squares.

2. Place a Fabric C square on the left side of a Fabric B rectangle, right sides together. Sew a thread-width below the drawn line, as shown.

3. Trim the seam allowance to ¼″. Open the top piece and press the seam toward the corner.

4. Repeat Steps 2 and 3 on the right end of the Fabric B rectangle.

5. Square the Flying Geese unit to 2″ × 3½″.

6. Repeat Steps 1–5 to make 48 Flying Geese units.

ASSEMBLE THE CORNER BLOCKS

1. Arrange 1 Fabric A square, 4 Flying Geese units, and 4 Fabric B squares as shown. Stitch together in 3 rows. Press the seams in Rows 1 and 3 to the outside and the seams in Row 2 to the inside.

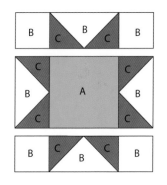

2. Sew the rows together. Press the seams open to reduce bulk. Square the corner block to 6½″ × 6½″.

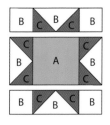

3. Repeat Steps 1 and 2 to make 12 corner blocks.

MAKE THE SASHING

1. Cut 34 strips 2½″ × 16½″ from Fabric B.

2. Cut 17 strips 2½″ × 16½″ from Fabric C.

3. Lay out 2 B strips and 1 C strip as shown. Stitch the strips together along the long edges (see Strip Piecing, page 5). Press the seams toward the Fabric C strip. Repeat this step to make 17 sashing strip sets.

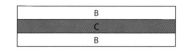

ASSEMBLE THE QUILT

1. Lay out 6 blocks and 9 sashing strip sets as shown. Stitch the blocks and sashing strip sets together to form 3 rows. Press the seams toward the sashing strip sets.

2. Arrange 3 corner blocks and 2 sashing strip sets as shown. Stitch together and press the seams toward the sashing. Make 4.

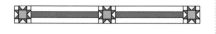

3. Lay out the sashing/corner block rows from Step 2 and the sashing/block rows from Step 1 as shown. Stitch the rows together. Press the seams toward the sashing/corner block rows.

BORDER

1. Cut 7 strips 2½" × width of fabric from Fabric A. Stitch the strips together end to end.

2. Measure the quilt top from top to bottom through the middle. Cut 2 strips to this length. Sew a strip to either side of the quilt. Press the seams toward the border.

3. Measure the quilt top from side to side across the middle, including borders added in Step 2. Cut 2 strips to this length. Sew a strip to the top and bottom of the quilt. Press the seams toward the border.

QUILTING

Layer the backing, batting, and quilt top. Quilt as desired.

BINDING

1. Cut 8 strips 2" × width of fabric (selvage to selvage) from the binding fabric.

2. Bind the quilt (see Making a Double-Fold Binding, page 6).

Photo by Photospin

Photo by Avalon

Photo by Avalon

Garden Cottage

This classic, relaxed house invites you in, promising secrets and romance—and, of course, a garden. The couple living here has created a haven of fragrant flowers, grasses, and bushes that charm in all seasons. It is a refuge from the busy world, the perfect place to spend an afternoon with a good book and a cool drink. The buzz of the bees, the song of the birds, and the flutter of a turning page are often all that is heard in this peaceful retreat. The colors of the garden are reflected in the quilt.

Designed and pieced by Ellen Murphy, quilted by Jennifer Cunningham

Finished quilt: 56½″ × 70½″

Finished block: 12″ × 12″

MATERIALS

Fabric A (white): 2⅜ yards

Fabric B (pink): ½ yard

Fabric C (yellow): 1⅛ yards

Fabric D (blue): 1⅛ yards

Fabric E (purple): ⅓ yard

Fabric F (green): ½ yard

Backing: 3⅔ yards (or 1¾ yards extra-wide quilt backing)

Batting: 64″ × 78″

Binding (green): ⅝ yard

BLOCK 1

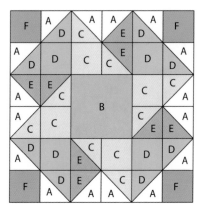

CUTTING

Fabric A
- Cut 48 squares 3¼″ × 3¼″.

Fabric B
- Cut 6 squares 4½″ × 4½″.

Fabric C
- Cut 24 squares 2½″ × 2½″.
- Cut 24 squares 3¼″ × 3¼″.

Fabric D
- Cut 24 squares 2½″ × 2½″.
- Cut 24 squares 3¼″ × 3¼″.

Fabric E
- Cut 24 squares 3¼″ × 3¼″.

Fabric F
- Cut 24 squares 2½″ × 2½″.

MAKE THE HALF-SQUARE TRIANGLES

1. Draw a diagonal line from corner to corner on the wrong side of 48 Fabric A 3¼″ squares. Repeat with 24 Fabric C 3¼″ squares.

2. Pair the 3¼″ × 3¼″ squares with right sides together in the following combinations: 12 A/C, 24 A/D, 12 A/E, and 12 E/C.

3. Stitch ¼″ from either side of the drawn line of each pair. Cut on the drawn line.

4. Press the seams of the half-square triangles as follows:

- Press the A/C half-square triangles toward Fabric C.

- Press 24 of the A/D half-square triangles toward Fabric A and the remaining 24 A/D half-square triangles toward Fabric D.

- Press the A/E half-square triangles toward Fabric A.

- Press the E/C half-square triangles toward Fabric E.

5. Square each half-square triangle to 2½″ × 2½″.

MAKE THE CORNER UNITS

1. Lay out the pieces for the corner units as shown in Step 2. Note the direction of the seam allowances in the A/D half-square triangles. This will help your piecing be more precise (see Locking the Seams, page 5).

2. Stitch the pieces together in 2 rows. Press the seam in Row 1 to the left and the seam in Row 2 to the right.

3. Stitch the rows together. Press the seam toward the bottom of the corner unit.

4. Square the corner unit to 4½" × 4½".

5. Repeat Steps 1–4 to make 24 corner units.

MAKE THE SIDE UNITS

1. Lay out the pieces for the side units as shown in Step 2.

2. Stitch the pieces together in 2 rows. Press the seam in Row 1 to the left and the seam in Row 2 to the right.

3. Stitch the rows together. Press the seam toward the top of the side unit.

4. Square the side unit to 4½" × 4½".

5. Repeat Steps 1–4 to make 24 side units.

ASSEMBLE BLOCK 1

1. Lay out 4 corner units, 4 side units, and a 4½" B square as shown. Refer to the illustration (below) to see how to rotate each corner and side unit. Stitch the units together in 3 rows. Press the seams in Rows 1 and 3 to the outside and the seams in Row 2 to the inside.

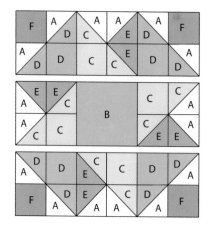

2. Stitch the rows together. Press the seams open to reduce bulk.

3. Square the block to 12½" × 12½".

4. Repeat Steps 1–3 to make 6 of Block 1.

BLOCK 2

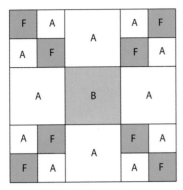

CUTTING

Fabric A

- Cut 24 squares 4½″ × 4½″.

- Cut 48 squares 2½″ × 2½″.

Fabric B

- Cut 6 squares 4½″ × 4½″.

Fabric F

- Cut 48 squares 2½″ × 2½″.

MAKE THE CORNER UNITS

1. Lay out 2 Fabric A 2½″ squares and 2 Fabric F 2½″ squares as shown. Stitch the squares together in 2 rows. Press the seam in Row 1 to the left and the seam in Row 2 to the right.

2. Stitch the rows together. Press the seam open to reduce bulk.

3. Repeat Steps 1 and 2 to make 24 corner units.

ASSEMBLE BLOCK 2

1. Lay out a Fabric B 4½″ square, 4 corner units, and 4 Fabric A 4½″ squares. Be sure to rotate the corner units as shown. Stitch them together in 3 rows. Press the seams in Rows 1 and 3 to the inside and the seams in Row 2 to the outside.

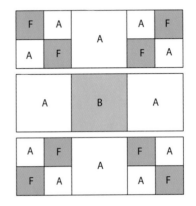

2. Stitch the rows together. Press the seams open to reduce bulk.

3. Square the block to 12½″ × 12½″.

4. Repeat Steps 1–3 to make 6 of Block 2.

QUILT CENTER

SASHING

1. Cut 31 strips 2½″ × 12½″ from Fabric A for sashing. Cut 20 squares 2½″ × 2½″ from Fabric B for cornerstones.

2. Arrange the blocks and Fabric A sashing strips into 2 rows as shown. Lay out 2 of each row. Stitch each row together and press the seams toward the sashing.

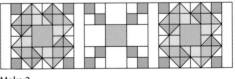

Make 2.

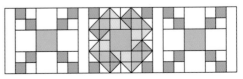

Make 2.

3. Sew the cornerstones and sashing strips together as shown. Press the seams toward the cornerstones. Repeat this step to make 5 cornerstone/sashing rows.

ASSEMBLE THE QUILT CENTER

Lay out 4 rows from Step 2 of Sashing (page 42) and 5 rows from Step 3 of Sashing (above), as shown. Pin and stitch the rows together, matching seams. Press the seams toward the cornerstone/sashing rows.

BORDERS

INNER BORDER

1. Cut 8 strips 2½″ × width of fabric from Fabric C. Cut 8 strips 2½″ × width of fabric from Fabric D.

2. Lay out the strips as shown. Stitch together along the long edges (see Strip Piecing, page 5). Make 2 strip-pieced units. Press the seams toward Fabric C.

Make 2.

3. Square up a side of a strip set and cross cut 14 strips, each 2½″ wide. Repeat this step with the remaining strip set.

4. Use a seam ripper to divide a strip from Step 3 into a set of 5 squares and a set of 2 squares. One square will be remaining. Repeat this step with 3 additional strips from Step 3, noting the color placement as shown.

Make 2.

Make 2.

5. Join the units from Steps 3 and 4 as shown. Make 2 of each.

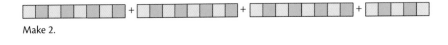

Make 2.

Make 2.

6. Stitch together 1 of each type of strip from Step 5 so the squares form a checkerboard pattern, as shown. Repeat this step to make a second checkerboard border.

7. Pin and sew a border from Step 6 to either side of the quilt.

8. Lay out 3 strip-pieced sets from Step 3 and a 2-square unit from Step 4 as shown. Stitch together. Repeat to make a total of 4.

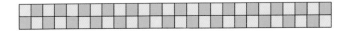

9. Pin and stitch together 2 strips from Step 8. Rotate 1 strip so that the squares make a checkerboard pattern as shown. Repeat with the remaining 2 strips from Step 8.

10. Pin the borders from Step 9 to the top and bottom of the quilt, matching the seams. Stitch the borders in place.

OUTER BORDER

1. Cut 7 strips 2″ × width of fabric from Fabric A. Stitch the strips together end to end.

2. Measure the quilt top from top to bottom through the middle. Cut 2 strips from the long strip formed in Step 1 to this length. Sew a strip to either side of the quilt.

3. Measure the quilt top from side to side through the middle, including outer borders added in Step 2. Cut 2 strips from the long strip formed in Step 1 to this length. Sew 1 strip to the top and 1 strip to the bottom of the quilt top.

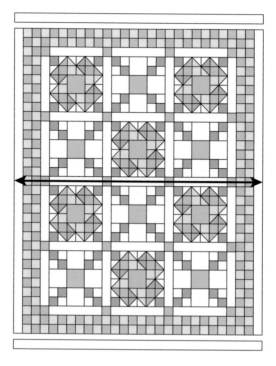

QUILTING

Layer the backing, batting, and quilt top. Quilt as desired.

BINDING

1. Cut 7 strips 2″ × width of fabric (selvage to selvage) from the binding fabric.

2. Bind the quilt (see Making the Double-Fold Binding, page 6).

Photo by Photospin

Photo by Avalon

Photo by Avalon

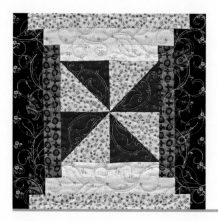

Cabin in the Woods

From cross-country skiing in the winter to catching fireflies in the summer, the family who lives here has worked hard to build an outdoorsy, close-to-nature lifestyle. They chose a spot near the babbling brook to build their cabin and cleared as few pines as possible, because they are dedicated to sound forest management practices. They used the wood that they cut in the cabin's construction. Then they brought the feeling of the land inside with a green and brown color scheme, knotty pine furnishings, a stone fireplace, and a quilt inspired by the trees and the windmills that speak to using the bounty of nature well. It all adds up to a warm and cozy home that's hard to leave, even for the adventures of the great outdoors.

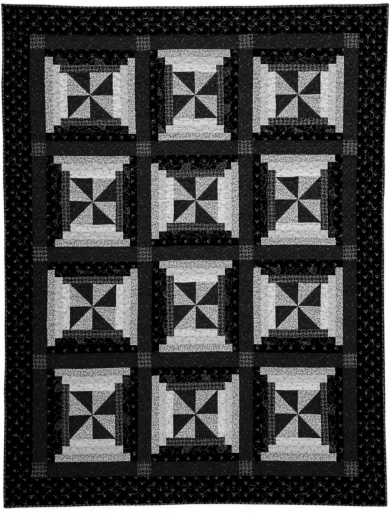

Designed and pieced by Ellen Murphy, quilted by Elaine Reed

Finished quilt: 51½″ × 65½″

Finished block: 12″ × 12″

MATERIALS

Fabric A (light #1): ¼ yard

Fabric B (light #2): ⅓ yard

Fabric C (light #3): 1 yard

Fabric D (gold): ⅝ yard

Fabric E (green): ½ yard

Fabric F (blue): 1⅜ yards

Fabric G (red): 1⅝ yards

Backing: 3⅓ yards (or 1¾ yards extra-wide quilt backing)

Batting: 59″ × 73″

Binding (gold): ½ yard

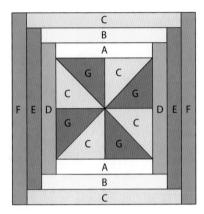

CUTTING

Fabric A
■ Cut 24 strips 1½″ × 6½″.

Fabric B
■ Cut 24 strips 1½″ × 8½″.

Fabric C
■ Cut 24 strips 1½″ × 10½″.

■ Cut 24 squares 4¼″ × 4¼″.

Fabric D
■ Cut 24 strips 1½″ × 8½″.

■ Cut 20 squares 2½″ × 2½″.

Fabric E
■ Cut 24 strips 1½″ × 10½″.

Fabric F
■ Cut 24 strips 1½″ × 12½″ strips.

Fabric G
■ Cut 24 squares 4¼″ × 4¼″.

■ Cut 31 strips 2½″ × 12½″.

MAKE THE HALF-SQUARE TRIANGLES

1. Draw a diagonal line from corner to corner on the wrong side of 24 Fabric C squares.

2. Place a Fabric C square and a Fabric G square right sides together. Stitch ¼″ from each side of the drawn line. Cut on the drawn line and press the seam toward Fabric C.

3. Square each half-square triangle to 3½″ × 3½″.

4. Repeat Steps 1–3 to make 48 C/G half-square triangles.

MAKE THE CENTER PINWHEELS

1. Lay out the half-square triangles as shown and stitch together in 2 rows. Press the seam in Row 1 to the left and the seam in Row 2 to the right.

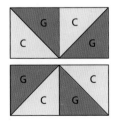

2. Sew the rows together. Press the seam open to reduce bulk.

3. Square the pinwheel to 6½" × 6½".

4. Repeat Steps 1–3 to make 12 pinwheels.

ASSEMBLE THE BLOCKS

1. Sew a Fabric A strip to the top and bottom of the pinwheel unit. Press the seams toward Fabric A. Sew a Fabric D strip to each side of the unit. Press the seams toward Fabric D. Continue in this manner, adding additional strips in the following order: B, E, C, and F. Refer to the illustration (below) for placement.

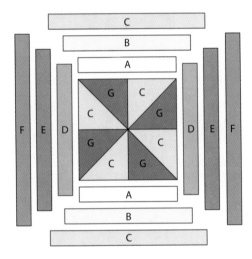

2. Square the block to 12½" × 12½".

3. Repeat Steps 1 and 2 to complete 12 blocks.

SASHING AND CORNERSTONES

1. Lay out the blocks so there are 3 across and 4 down. Rotate every other block as shown.

2. Sew a Fabric G strip between the blocks in a row as shown. Add another Fabric G sashing strip to either end of the row. Press the seams toward Fabric G. Make 4.

3. Stitch 3 Fabric G strips and 4 Fabric D squares together as shown. Press the seams toward Fabric G. Make 5.

4. Arrange the rows from Steps 2 and 3 as shown. Pin and stitch them together, matching the seams. Press the seams toward the narrow rows of sashing.

BORDER

1. Cut 6 strips 4" × width of fabric from Fabric F. Stitch the strips together end to end.

2. Measure the quilt top from top to bottom through the middle. Cut 2 strips to this length. Stitch a strip to either side of the quilt. Press the seams toward the borders.

3. Measure the quilt top from side to side, including the side borders. Cut 2 strips to this length. Stitch a strip to the top and bottom of the quilt. Press the seam toward the borders.

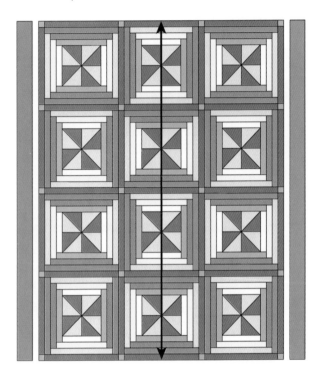

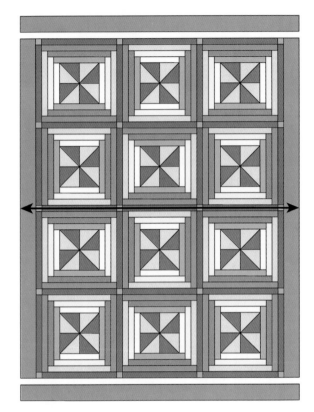

QUILTING

Layer the backing, batting, and quilt top. Quilt as desired.

BINDING

1. Cut 6 strips 2″ × width of fabric (selvage to selvage) from the binding fabric.

2. Bind the quilt (see Making a Double-Fold Binding, page 6).

Vintage Bungalow

Vintage now, bungalows were the bee's knees when first built in the western United States. Simple and straightforward, they were functional and much smaller than the styles that preceded them. They allowed for the expansion of the suburbs and high-density neighborhoods. This bungalow's residents are still quite practical. They love the age, character, and quality workmanship of their eclectic home. They never miss the weekend flea markets, and scour the stalls for just the right pieces. From vintage kitchenware to retro furniture—if they love it, they can make it work here. This quilt design was inspired by one of their antique stained-glass windows.

Designed and pieced by Ellen Murphy, quilted by Jennifer Cunningham
Fabric from the Vintage Modern collection by Bonnie and Camille for Moda

Finished quilt: 45½" × 65½"

Fabric A (red): 1⅛ yards

Fabric B (pink): ⅝ yard

Fabric C (turquoise): ⅝ yard

Fabric D (large floral): 1⅛ yards

Fabric E (green): ¾ yard

Fabric F (light turquoise): 1¼ yards

Assorted fabrics: 16 squares 4⅜″ × 4⅜″ for yo-yos

Backing: 3 yards (or 1½ yards extra-wide quilt backing)

Batting: 53″ × 73″

Binding: ⅝ yard

Large Clover yo-yo maker (optional)

16 assorted buttons: approximately 1″ wide (optional)

MAKE THE CENTER MEDALLION

CUTTING

Fabric A
- Cut 4 squares 4¼″ × 4¼″.
- Cut 12 squares 3½″ × 3½″.
- Cut 1 square 6½″ × 6½″.

Fabric B
- Cut 8 squares 4¼″ × 4¼″.
- Cut 4 rectangles 3½″ × 6½″.

Fabric C
- Cut 4 rectangles 3½″ × 6½″.
- Cut 8 squares 3½″ × 3½″.

Fabric D
- Cut 4 rectangles 3½″ × 6½″.

Fabric E
- Cut 16 squares 3½″ × 3½″.
- Cut 4 squares 4¼″ × 4¼″.

MAKE THE HALF-SQUARE TRIANGLES

1. Draw a diagonal line from corner to corner on the wrong side of 8 Fabric B squares.

2. Pair the 4¼″ × 4¼″ squares with right sides together in the following combinations: 4 A/B pairs and 4 B/E pairs.

3. Stitch ¼″ from each side of the drawn line of a pair. Cut on the drawn line and press the seams toward the darker fabric. Square to 3½″ × 3½″. Repeat this step to make 8 A/B half-square triangles and 8 B/E half-square triangles.

MAKE THE CORNER UNITS

1. Arrange squares and half-square triangles as shown. Stitch them together in 3 rows. Press the seams in Rows 1 and 3 to the outside and the seams in Row 2 to the inside.

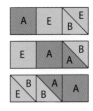

2. Stitch the rows together and press the seams toward the top. Square the corner unit to 9½″ × 9½″.

3. Repeat Steps 1 and 2 to make 4 corner units.

MAKE THE FLYING GEESE UNITS

1. Draw a diagonal line from corner to corner on the wrong side of 8 Fabric E 3½″ × 3½″ squares and 8 Fabric C squares.

2. Place a Fabric E 3½″ × 3½″ square on the left side of a Fabric C 3½″ × 6½″ rectangle as shown. Sew a thread-width above the drawn line.

3. Trim the seam ¼″ outside the stitching. Open the top piece and press the seam toward the corner.

4. Repeat Steps 2 and 3 on the right side of the rectangle.

5. Square the Flying Geese unit to 3½″ × 6½″.

6. Repeat Steps 2–5 to make 4 Flying Geese units using Fabrics C and E.

7. Repeat Steps 2–5 to make 4 Flying Geese units as shown, using the Fabric C squares and the Fabric B rectangles.

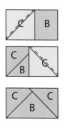

MAKE THE OUTER MIDDLE UNITS

1. Lay out 2 Flying Geese units and a Fabric D rectangle as shown. Stitch them together along the long edges, taking care with the Flying Geese points.

2. Press the seams toward the bottom of the unit. Square the unit to 6½″ × 9½″.

3. Repeat Steps 1 and 2 to make 4 outer middle units.

ASSEMBLE THE CENTER MEDALLION

1. Lay out 4 corner units and 4 outer middle units as shown, placing a Fabric A 6½″ square in the middle. Stitch the pieces together to form 3 rows. Press the seams in Rows 1 and 3 to the outside and the seams in Row 2 to the inside.

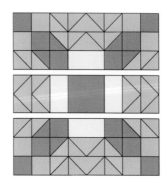

2. Stitch the rows together and press the seams open to reduce bulk. Square to 24½″ × 24½″.

BORDERS

FIRST INNER BORDER

1. Cut 4 strips 6½″ × 24½″ from Fabric D.

2. Cut 4 squares 6½″ × 6½″ from Fabric A.

3. Sew a Fabric D strip from Step 1 to each side of the center medallion. Press the seams to the outside.

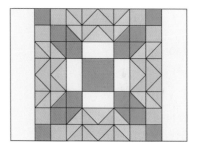

4. Sew a Fabric A square from Step 2 to each end of the remaining Fabric D strips from Step 1. Press the seams toward the Fabric D strips.

5. Sew a unit from Step 4 to the top and bottom of the center unit. Press the seams open to reduce bulk.

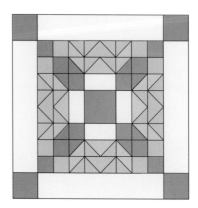

MAKE THE POINTED UNITS FOR THE BORDERS

CUTTING

Fabric A

- Cut 32 squares 2¾" × 2¾".
- Cut 2 strips 2½" × 36½".

Fabric B

- Cut 8 rectangles 5" × 6½".

Fabric C

- Cut 8 rectangles 5" × 6½".

Fabric E

- Cut 2 strips 2½" × 36½".

Assemble the Pointed Border Units

1. Draw a line from corner to corner on the wrong side of 32 Fabric A squares.

2. Place a Fabric A square in the upper left corner of a Fabric B rectangle as shown. Stitch a thread-width above the drawn line.

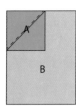

3. Trim ¼" outside the seamline. Open the top piece and press toward the corner.

4. Repeat Steps 2 and 3 to add another Fabric A square in the upper right corner as shown.

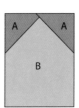

5. Trim the unit to 5" × 6½".

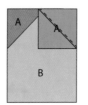

6. Repeat Steps 2–5 to make 8 units.

7. Repeat Steps 2–5 to make 8 units using Fabric C rectangles in place of the Fabric B rectangles.

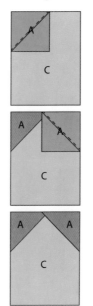

8. Lay out the pointed units in a row as shown and stitch them together. Press the seams open.

9. Add a Fabric A strip to the top of the row and a Fabric E strip to the bottom.

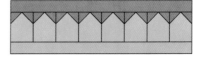

10. Repeat Steps 8 and 9 to assemble the other pointed border unit.

11. Sew a unit from Step 10 to the top and bottom of the center unit as shown.

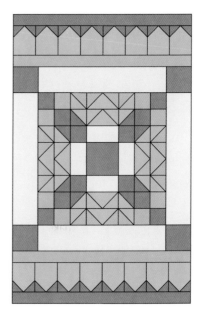

OUTER BORDER

1. Cut 6 strips 5″ × width of fabric from Fabric F. Stitch the strips together end to end.

2. Measure the quilt top from top to bottom through the middle. Cut 2 strips to this length. Stitch a strip to either side of the quilt. Press the seams toward the outer borders.

3. Measure the quilt top from side to side through the middle, including the borders added in Step 2. Cut 2 strips to this length. Stitch a strip to the top and bottom of the quilt.

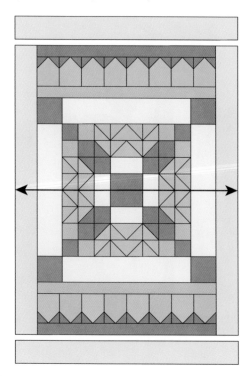

MAKE THE YO-YOS

Using the 16 assorted 4⅜″ squares and a large Clover yo-yo maker, make 16 yo-yos according to the manufacturer's directions. *Set aside.*

If you do not have a yo-yo maker, cut a 4″ circle from each of the assorted 4⅜″ squares. Sew a basting stitch around the outside of each circle approximately ⅛″ from the edge. Pull the basting thread tails to gather the circle. Tie the thread to secure; then press to flatten the yo-yo.

QUILTING

Layer the backing, batting, and quilt top. Quilt as desired.

BINDING

1. Cut 7 strips 2″ × width of fabric (selvage to selvage) from the binding fabric.

2. Bind the quilt (see Making a Double-Fold Binding, page 6).

FINISHING

Sew a yo-yo at the tip of each pointed unit in the top and bottom borders as shown. Add a button to the center of each yo-yo if you wish.

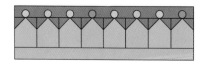

Photo by Shutterstock

Photo by Avalon

Photo by Avalon

Craftsman Home

Designed and pieced by Ellen Murphy, quilted by Elaine Reed

On a quiet lane, this Craftsman home feels both elegant and comfortable. It radiates a cozy homeyness and is indeed home to a lively family. The entire family enjoys being outdoors and participating in community events, but their favorite activity is restoring the cottage to its original look. They search out local, natural materials and authentic handcrafted decor and accessories to enhance their home's vintage feel. This quilt is inspired by an Arts and Crafts–style lighting fixture that they found at an estate auction.

Finished quilt: 59½″ × 74″
Finished block: 10″ × 10″

MATERIALS

Fabric A (white): 3 yards

Fabric B (gold): ⅞ yard

Fabric C (turquoise): 1⅛ yards

Fabric D (rust): 1⅝ yards

Backing: 4⅝ yards (or 2 yards extra-wide quilt backing)

Batting: 67″ × 82″

Binding: ⅝ yard

MAKE THE BLOCKS

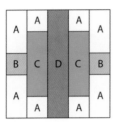

CUTTING

Fabric A

- Cut 48 squares 2½″ × 2½″.

- Cut 48 rectangles 2½″ × 4½″.

Fabric B

- Cut 24 squares 2½″ × 2½″.

Fabric C

- Cut 24 rectangles 2½″ × 6½″.

Fabric D

- Cut 12 rectangles 2½″ × 10½″.

1. Stitch a Fabric A rectangle to the top and bottom of a Fabric B square as shown. Press the seams toward Fabric B. Repeat to make 24 units.

2. Lay out 2 Fabric A squares and a Fabric C rect-angle as shown and stitch together. Press the seams toward Fabric C. Repeat to make 24 units.

3. Sew a unit from Step 2 to either side of a Fabric D rectangle. Press the seams toward the center.

4. Stitch a unit from Step 1 to either side of the unit from Step 3. Press the seams toward the center. Square the block to 10½″ × 10½″.

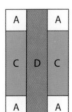

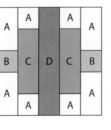

5. Repeat Steps 3 and 4 to make 12 blocks.

MAKE THE CORNER BLOCKS

CUTTING

Fabric A

- Cut 80 squares 2″ × 2″.

Fabric B

- Cut 20 squares 2″ × 2″.

Fabric C

- Cut 80 squares 2″ × 2″.

1. Lay out all of the squares and sew them together in 3 rows as shown. Press the seams in Rows 1 and 3 to the inside and the seams in Row 2 to the outside.

2. Sew the rows together. Press the seams open to reduce bulk.

3. Square the corner block to 5″ × 5″.

4. Repeat Steps 1–3 to make 20 corner blocks.

ASSEMBLE THE QUILT

1. Cut 31 rectangles 5″ × 10½″ from Fabric A.

2. Lay out the blocks and sashing strips as shown. Stitch them together. Press the seams toward the blocks. Repeat to make 4 rows.

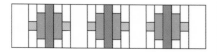

3. Lay out the corner blocks and sashing strips as shown. Stitch them together and press the seams toward the corner blocks. Make 5 rows.

4. Arrange the rows from Steps 2 and 3 as shown and stitch them together. Press the seams toward the corner block/sashing strips.

BORDERS

INNER BORDER

1. Cut 6 strips 1½″ × width of fabric from Fabric D. Stitch together end to end.

2. Measure the quilt from top to bottom through the middle. Cut 2 strips to this length. Sew a strip to either side of the quilt. Press the seams toward the border.

3. Measure the quilt top from side to side through the middle, including the borders added in Step 2. Cut 2 strips to this length. Stitch a strip to the top and bottom of the quilt. Press the seams toward the border.

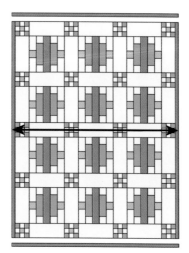

PIECED BORDER

CUTTING

Fabric A
- Cut 2 strips 3″ × width of fabric.
- Cut 4 rectangles 3″ × 4″.

Fabric B
- Cut 4 strips 2½″ × width of fabric.

Fabric C
- Cut 4 strips 2½″ × width of fabric.

Fabric D
- Cut 2 strips 2½″ × width of fabric.
- Cut 4 squares 4″ × 4″.

Make the Pieced Borders

1. Lay out the strips as shown and sew together (see Strip Piecing, page 5). Press the seams in 1 direction. Repeat to make another strip set.

A
B
C
D
C
B

2. Square up an edge, and then cut across the strip into 4″ sections. Repeat with the remaining strip set for a total of 18 sections 4″ wide.

3. Lay out the sections as shown, with 5 pieced units and 1 Fabric A rectangle. Stitch them together. Repeat to make 2 pieced side borders.

4. Measure the quilt from top to bottom across the middle. Trim the side pieced borders to match this length, cutting an equal amount from each end of the border. *Set aside.*

5. Lay out the remaining pieced sections and 1 Fabric A rectangle as shown. Sew together. Repeat this step to make 2 pieced borders for the top and bottom.

6. Measure the quilt top from side to side across the middle. Trim the top and bottom pieced borders to match this length, cutting an equal amount from each end of the border.

7. Sew a Fabric D square to each end of the top and bottom pieced borders from Step 6.

8. Stitch a pieced side border from Step 4 to either side of the quilt top. Stitch a border from Step 7 to the top and bottom of the quilt.

OUTER BORDER

1. Cut 7 strips 1½" × width of fabric from Fabric D. Stitch the strips together end to end.

2. Follow Steps 2 and 3 of Inner Border (page 61) to cut and stitch the outer borders to the quilt.

QUILTING

Layer the backing, batting, and quilt top. Quilt as desired.

BINDING

1. Cut 7 strips 2" × width of fabric (selvage to selvage) from the binding fabric.

2. Bind the quilt (see Making the Double-Fold Binding, page 6).

ABOUT THE AUTHOR

Photo by Avalon

Ellen Murphy says she was born with a crayon in her hand. She has loved art and design her entire life. Since she was a teenager, she has loved quilting and has always enjoyed manipulating fabric—whether for garment construction or craft pursuits. Ellen has a degree in fine art and has a love of color. Working in graphic design and as a quilting teacher helped her create patterns that are easy to understand.

Ellen loves to travel, and that love has taken her around the world. She brings the inspiration she receives from her journeys to her designs. Ellen is the owner and designer of American Homestead, a craft pattern design company. See what Ellen is up to at www.americanhomesteaddesign.com or www.americanhomestead.blogspot.com.

Great Titles *from* C&T PUBLISHING

Available at your local retailer or **www.ctpub.com** *or* **800.284.1114**

For a list of other fine books from C&T Publishing, visit our website to view our catalog online.

C&T PUBLISHING, INC.
P.O. Box 1456
Lafayette, CA 94549
800.284.1114

Email: ctinfo@ctpub.com
Website: www.ctpub.com

C&T Publishing's professional photography services are now available to the public. Visit us at www.ctmediaservices.com.

TIPS AND TECHNIQUES can be found at www.ctpub.com > Consumer Resources > Quiltmaking Basics: Tips & Techniques for Quiltmaking & More

For quilting supplies:

COTTON PATCH
1025 Brown Ave.
Lafayette, CA 94549
Store: 925.284.1177
Mail order: 925.283.7883

Email: CottonPa@aol.com
Website: www.quiltusa.com

Note: Fabrics shown may not be currently available, as fabric manufacturers keep most fabrics in print for only a short time.